AQUATIQUE

AQUATIQUE

PHOTOGRAPHS BY BRIAN OGLESBEE

Foreword by Lesley Brill

INSIGHT EDITIONS

San Rafael, California

I was at an art show in New York City when I saw one of Brian Oglesbee's prints.
At the same time I spotted a noted gallery owner I know and I said, "Did you see that print?"
The answer was "Yeah," but without a great deal of enthusiasm.
I said, "I know you looked at it, but did you see it?"
"Yes, of course I did."
"No, you didn't," I said.
"What the hell are you talking about? I said I saw it!"
"No. You looked at it but you didn't see it!"
And with that I grabbed his wrist and dragged him up close,
where the multiplicity of images within images were visible.
The response was: "Oh... my... God... now I see it!"
Look closely at Brian's work.
It brings great rewards
(even if it's only black & white).

—Jay Maisel

CONTENTS

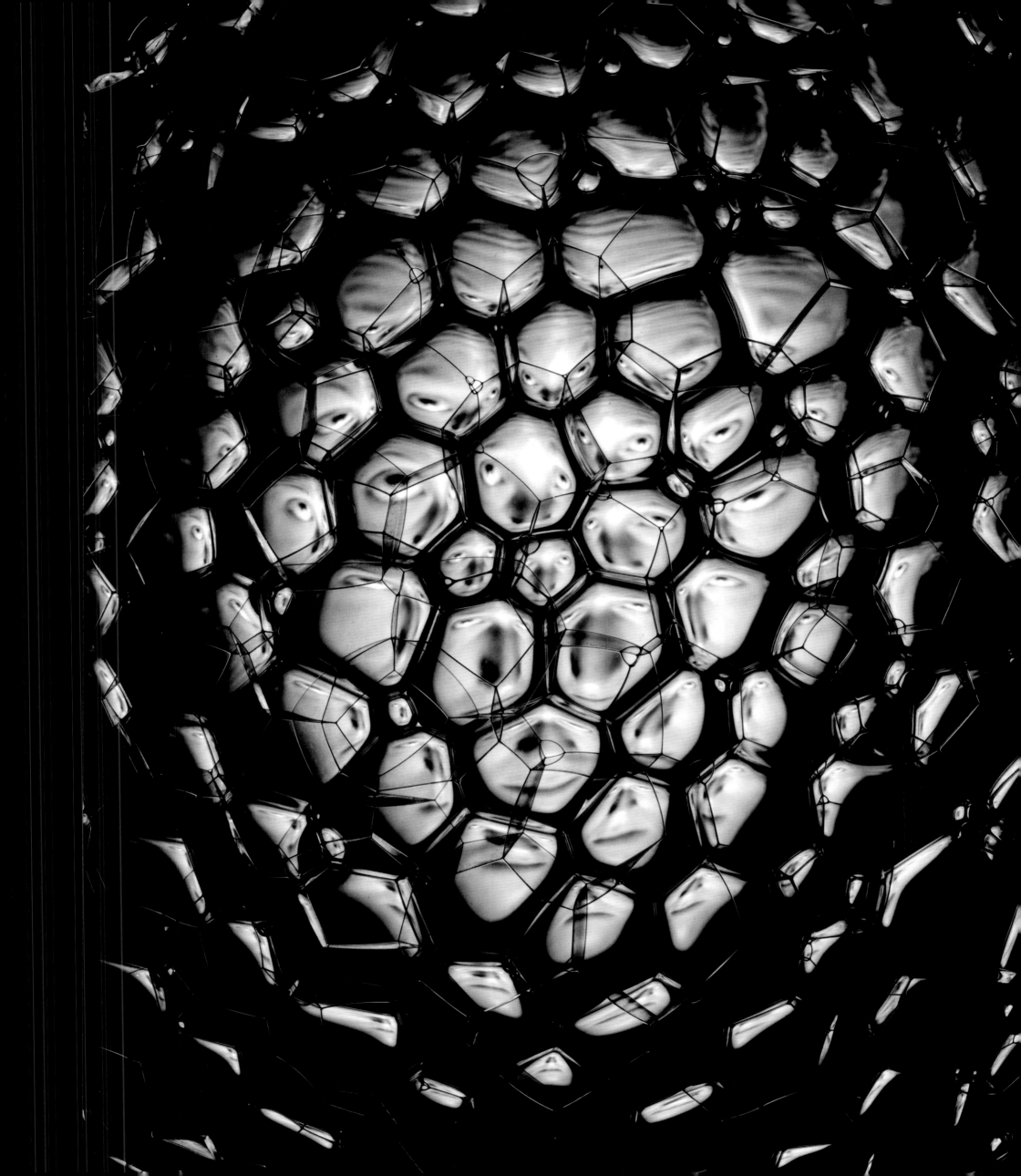

FOREWORD

The exuberant beauty of Brian Oglesbee's *Aquatique* springs from its fascinated joy in creation. Its photos flow with energy as abundantly as with water. The universe and the images themselves are born together; the workings of imagination and its outcomes appear simultaneously. Human figures create the world and come into being at the same time; they are goddesses and gods, and the spawn of gods and goddesses; they are feminine and androgynous; they are at once themselves in particular and all humanity collectively. *Aquatique* fuses its archetypal images with those of everyone who dreams. True to the special capabilities of photography, Oglesbee's camera meticulously records all that exists before it and makes visible the All in which it exists.

Life begins in rebirth, for life is replication; and understanding begins with perceiving again, in recognition. Creation, then, must be re-creation (and, happily, recreation).

Absent stories or allusions, Oglesbee's photographs nonetheless feel intensely mythic. All depict metamorphosis, the fluid exchange between self and other, one and many, now and then. Irving Massey wrote that metamorphosis is the process through which one "is reborn by himself... a process of change essentially unaccompanied by language."[1] Oglesbee has said of his work, "The picture begins where the words leave off."[2] *Aquatique* renders rebirth visible; we see without linguistic mediation the inexplicable, inevitable process of becoming— what Massey called "the form in which our encroachment on the future is made tangible."[3]

In making these pictures, Oglesbee goes where the motives of creation lead, where the spirit moves. Like Edward Weston, an early influence, Oglesbee meditates on energy and a universe in which form and force are one. A color still life that he made in the early 1980s bears the title of the physicists' Holy Grail, "Grand Unification." The bubbles and ripples of *Aquatique* provide images for the idea from quantum theory that in a void matter and energy wink spontaneously into and out of being. In *Aquatique* existence is a constant coming-out and trying-out, the expression not of destiny but of limitless possibility.

Direction-dimension in Oglesbee's photographs—as in the

time just after the Big Bang—is as nascent as matter-energy; over, under, around, and through are not yet wholly distinct.

The subjects of *Aquatique* are grand, cosmic. The prints, therefore, need to be big. They also need to be big because they contain multitudes at every scale. The fractal repetitions of Oglesbee's pictures stretch from the grain of sand in which Blake saw the universe to the strings of galaxies that are at present the farthest we can see.

Pure water can be seen only when it is stirred by gravity or impinging movement, which it, in return, makes visible. As with the creator and the created, energy and matter, the dancer and the dance, the visual equivalence between motion and water is entire and perfect.

The waters of *Aquatique* are the waters of life. Water is the most paradoxically enduring of humanity's symbols of change. Life is change, and you can never step again into the same stream you are crossing now. Water sweeps across, under, around, over, and through all boundaries. It refracts, reflects, and transmits light; it is the "universal solvent." Babies and most other earthly creatures swim into existence in a rich amniotic bath. Metaphorically, the fluidity and capaciousness of water more than equals its physical flow. It is the mind itself, "that ocean," poet Andrew Marvell wrote, "where each kind / Does straight his own resemblance find."

Like imagination, water unifies and synchronizes the multiplicities of matter, energy, space, and time. Oglesbee's photos achieve grand unification by revealing deeply shared identities without effacing differences; their elements are permeable to each other, not merely "like."

Oglesbee's photos comprehend experience simultaneously from outside and inside, on the level, from above, and from below. *Aquatique* imagines a universe not of either/or but of both/and. Among spirit, matter, and energy, *Aquatique* assumes an intimate connection. It shows us as human in the universe and the universe as human. Divinity signifies identity: *I am the world and the world is me.* Human in form, the gods of Oglesbee's photos are the remnants of original creation that can still be discovered in us. They are at once the shape of the Big Bang and its latest outcome. The fluid interchanges between the human and the cosmic are snapshots of the metamorphoses through which everything exists.

Oglesbee's pictures picture picturemaking. Like all works of art that enlarge us and our world, they meditate upon their means as well as their meanings. The two prove so closely related as to be scarcely distinguishable. *Aquatique* ingeniously exploits the resources of view camera, lighting and set, human form, black-and-white film, and paper. The vertical orientation of the prints crops our peripheral vision and puts the image in the middle of our sight, the acutest visual field, while the central placement of the figures further sharpens our focus on them.

The photos of *Aquatique* reward, indeed require, viewing distances from well back to very close. Fine detail and large design have equal importance. Oglesbee's pictures represent not only the truth of Lisette Model's idea that the more specific a photo is the more universal its meanings will be, but they also show one of the means—the object merging into its underlying form—through which that paradox may come to be true.

Without exception, the photos of *Aquatique* have the integrity conferred by unmanipulated printings of single, unretouched negatives. They figure forth photography's uniquely powerful grip on time, its ability at once to vividly represent change and to stop it. Unusually, however, Oglesbee's work captures not the moment in which present becomes past, but the instant that joins the present with the time to come, "the form in which our encroachment on the future is made tangible."

In all the prints of *Aquatique*, waves of water and light, bubbles, groupings of foliage and stones embrace figures whose gestures in turn shape their surroundings. Fertile waters bring the world and its spirits into existence, just as solutions of exotic chemicals give substance to the latent images of photosensitive film and paper.

Because he understands and securely controls his art, Oglesbee can afford to grant his photographic muses considerable autonomy. "I'm where I want to be," he has said, "when I'm where the picture takes over, where it dictates what gets done."

The spirit of the photo arises from interaction between the "facilitator" (the artist) and the work that participates in its own making. Part of that interaction includes bountiful play with what Oglesbee calls "literal truth and poetic truth." The photographs record without alteration what was within the field of view of the lens when they were exposed, but the worlds Oglesbee creates—often as elaborately constructed and illuminated as small movie sets—are designed to be paradoxical and richly expressive.

Complete and self-sufficient, Oglesbee's photographs ask only for thoughtful, engaged viewing. Among the aspects of *Aquatique* that await fuller discussion is the deftly paired sense of simultaneous wit and threat that presides, mildly but pervasively, in many of its images. Disturbances in the water and softening focus threaten dissolution. At the same time, the distortions of bubble, ripple, and soft focus have the comic appeal of funhouse mirrors.

None of Oglesbee's photographs are without threatening, ironic, and comic elements. Such perspectives, however, neither pervade them nor predominate. Rather, *Aquatique* has an objectivity, an innocent straightforwardness that is characteristic of the most primitive, simplest art—and the most sophisticated. Its photographs advance the expressive range of their medium while returning to, and renewing, the profoundest themes of all lasting meditations: life and consciousness, love, the sometimes grotesque beauty of humankind, the divinity of creation, the paradoxes and predicaments of being human in a world that simultaneously is and is not us.

—Lesley Brill

Lesley Brill has published essays on the photos of Arbus, Atget, and Brett Weston and books on the films of Hitchcock and John Huston. He teaches at Wayne State University in Detroit. His most recent book is Crowds, Power, and Transformation in Cinema *(Wayne State University Press, 2006).*

[1] Irving Massey, *The Gaping Pig: Literature and Metamorphosis* (Berkeley, Los Angeles, London: University of California Press, 1976), p. 52.

[2] All the quotations from Brian Oglesbee come from conversations that occurred during June, 1999.

[3] Massey, p. 52.

REFLECTIONS

*A*quatique presents a collection of photographic images from my *Water Series*, exploring the visual interaction of water and the human figure. For more than a decade, I have been experimenting in my studio with the optics of water and the potency of its visual metaphors.

Water is essential for the very presence of life. As a symbol, it is remarkably compelling and, when combined with an equally powerful icon, the human form, has allowed for a rich visual exploration to unfold.

In thinking about making pictures, I sometimes try to reduce things to primary elements. For instance, in one sense, making a still photograph represents morphing three dimensions (or four if you include time) into two by using a device that records patterns of light. A similar reduction for me, and a very important primary concept of the studio in photography, is that it's a place where you can have *no* light—and, of course, light is the most basic, universally important ingredient of the photographic image.

Photography itself seems to have two distinct modes. In one, the photographer goes out into the world of people, places, things, and events with a camera seeking matter to depict, selecting the subject of the photograph from the surroundings: a "subtractive" process. He or she composes the image by deciding what to *exclude*, not just what to include, in the frame.

The other mode is to start with nothing and build an image from light and subject in the studio. This "additive" process is how I make my pictures. Working in a place where "you can have no light" means that I am responsible for every beam that reaches the film and therefore everything that is visible in the final image. This I find challenging.

The *Water Series* began, innocently enough, as an attempt on my part to see if I could mimic nature in the studio. I had recently done a picture of objects floating in air above a figure. Looking at this image (which I now call "Water Series 00" – page 140), it came to mind that it might be interesting to see whether I could make a similar picture with the figure under water.

Never having tried to construct a natural-looking water scene in the studio before, I exercised my "reduce things to their most basic" philosophy and realized that in an optically important way we don't really "see" water. Water "mirrors" and "lenses," so that we can only see what is submersed in it, floating on it, refracted by it, or reflected in it. In nature, water is always moving, and its motion relative to the viewer and the light dictates what it does optically. The key is to control the elements which affect the shape of the surface of the water, to create the illusion of a pond, a stream—or a galaxy or a microcosm.

It occurred to me that what makes water look "natural" outdoors are the characteristics of its surface as it reflects the sky. Surface geometry is determined by wind, gravity, and mechanical disturbances (something swimming or splashing). I proceeded to make a set with water (and a "sky reflection" and a splash and some wind) to test my theory. Could I convincingly mimic nature in the studio?

I was pleased with the result ("Water Series 01") and began constructing larger-scale and more elaborate sets. During these early experiments, I had no plan to expand this exploration into a substantial series, and had no idea that I was embarking on a ten-year quest that would lead me to some rather surprising discoveries.

I have endeavored to analyze the optics of water as they relate to photographic image-making and to learn to control and manipulate them. Initially, my concern was to attempt to mimic nature convincingly. Along the way, I learned how to build sets and devices that allowed the creation of entirely otherworldly visual environments with wave forms, splashes, and fields of lensing bubbles.

My photographs are very "straight"; in other words, the camera simply records what was in front of it. All negatives are 4 × 5 inches. The light is generated by electronic flash. What is seen in the print is what was presented to the camera; there is no manipulation of the image after the initial single exposure.

In all but one of the photographs in *Aquatique*, the camera, or viewer, is on one side of the surface of the water and the figure is on the other. Sometimes the camera is above and sometimes below, yet it is always focused on the surface of the water, which I see as a metaphorical membrane, intended to symbolize that which separates—and binds—the physical and the spiritual.

—Brian Oglesbee
Wellsville, New York

WATER SERIES

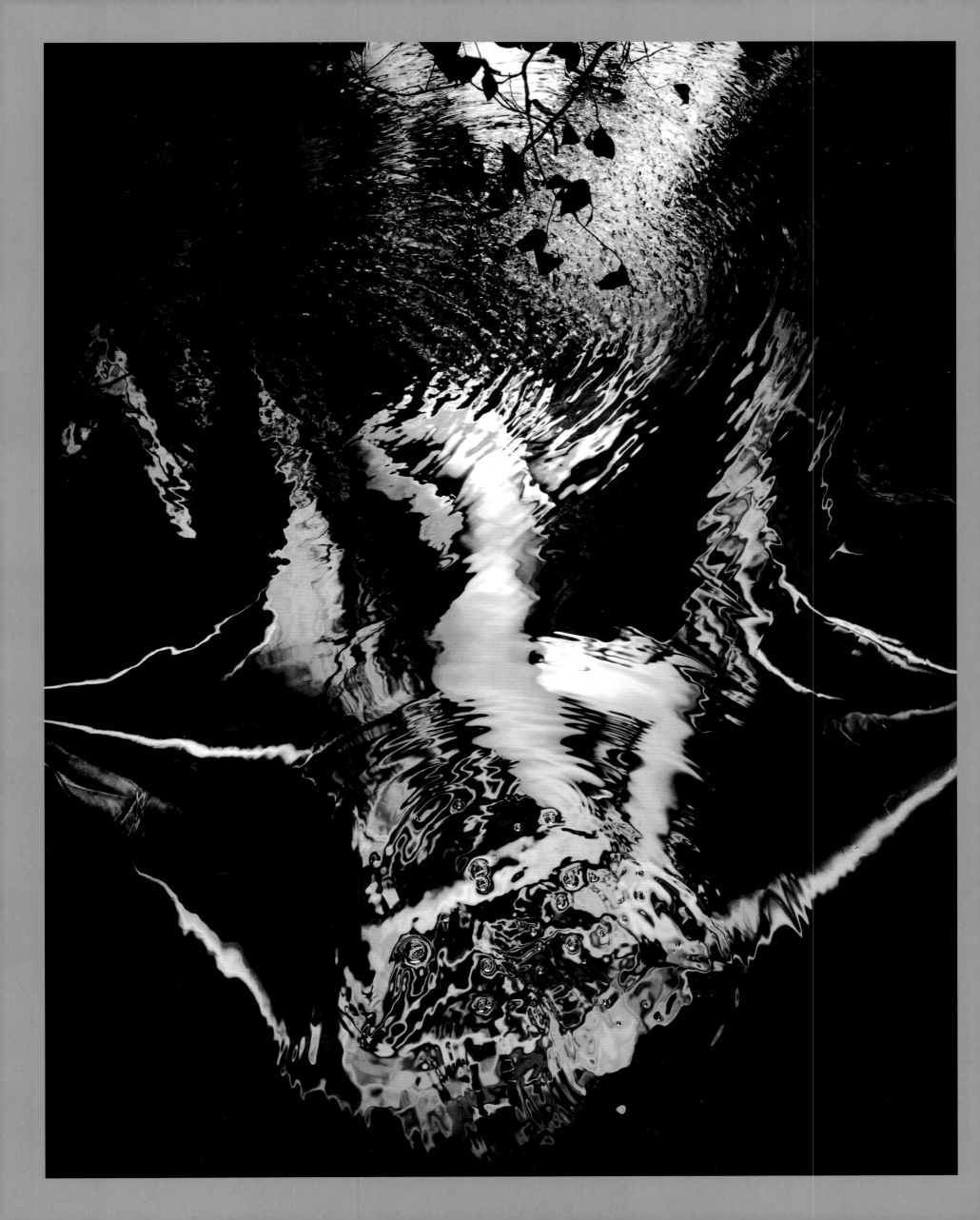

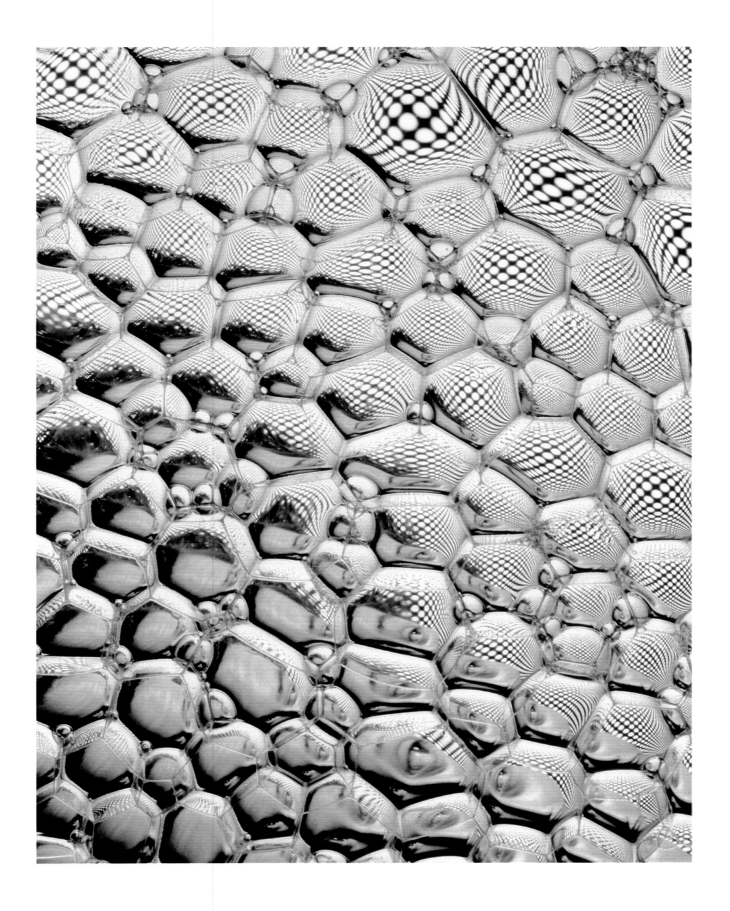

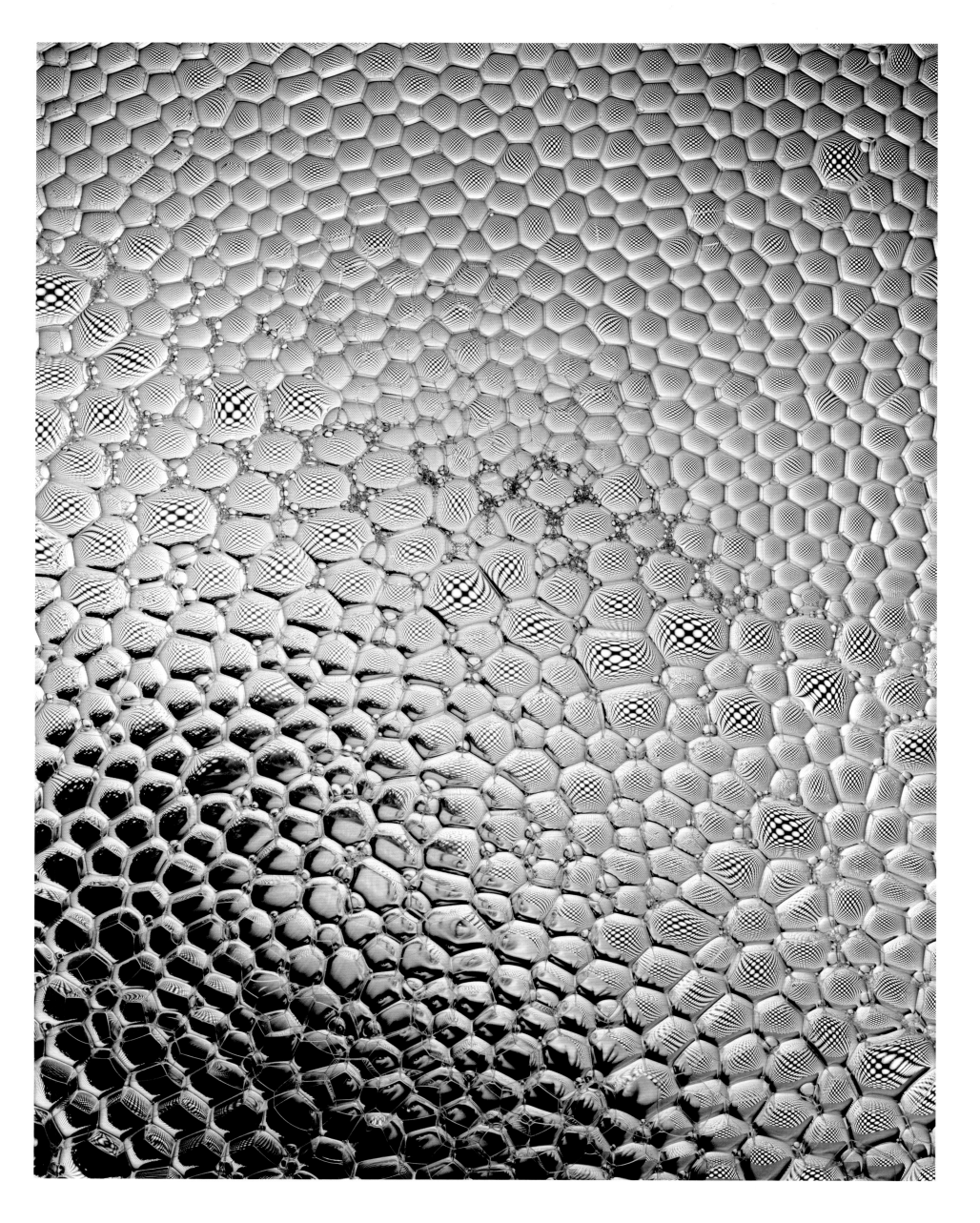

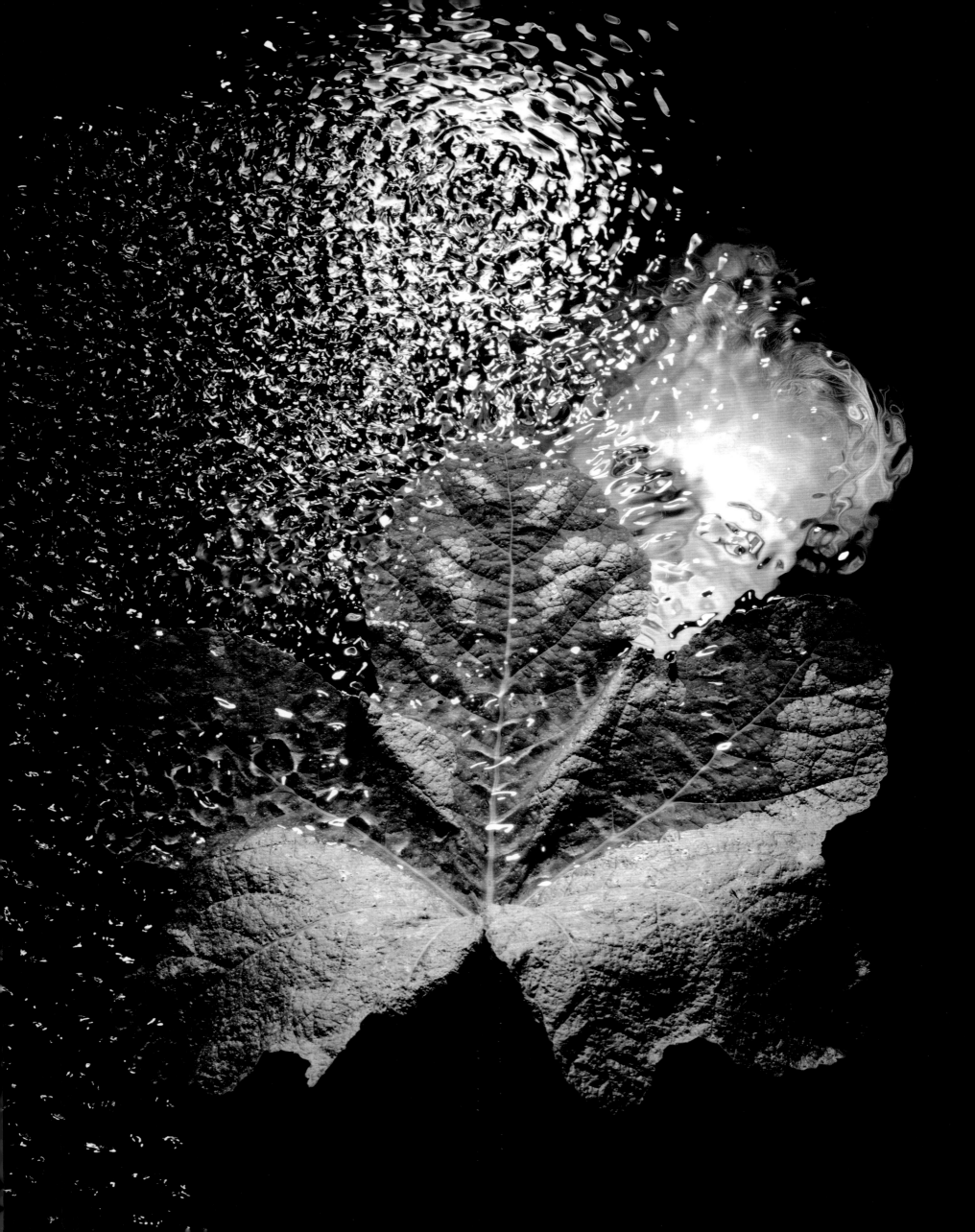

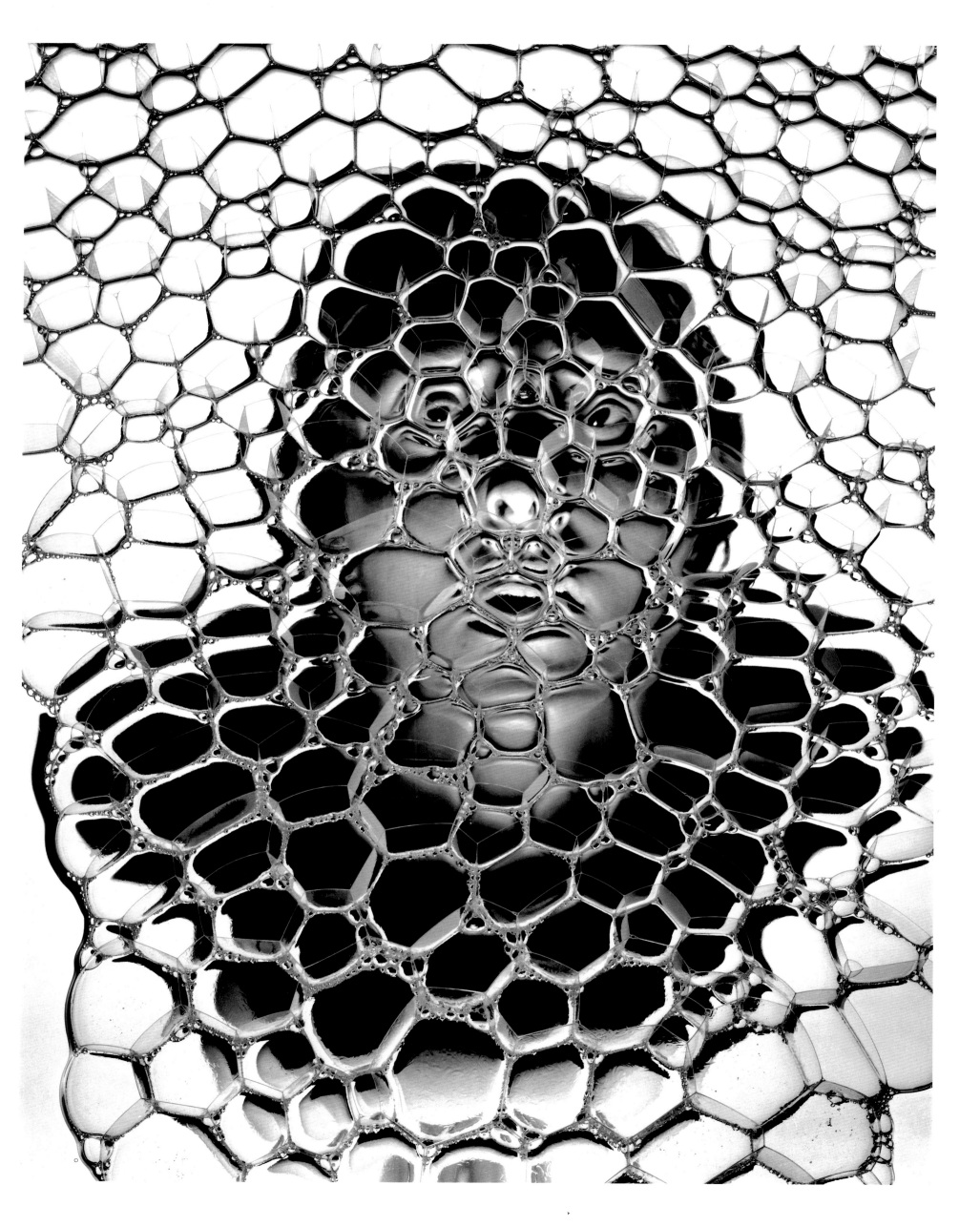

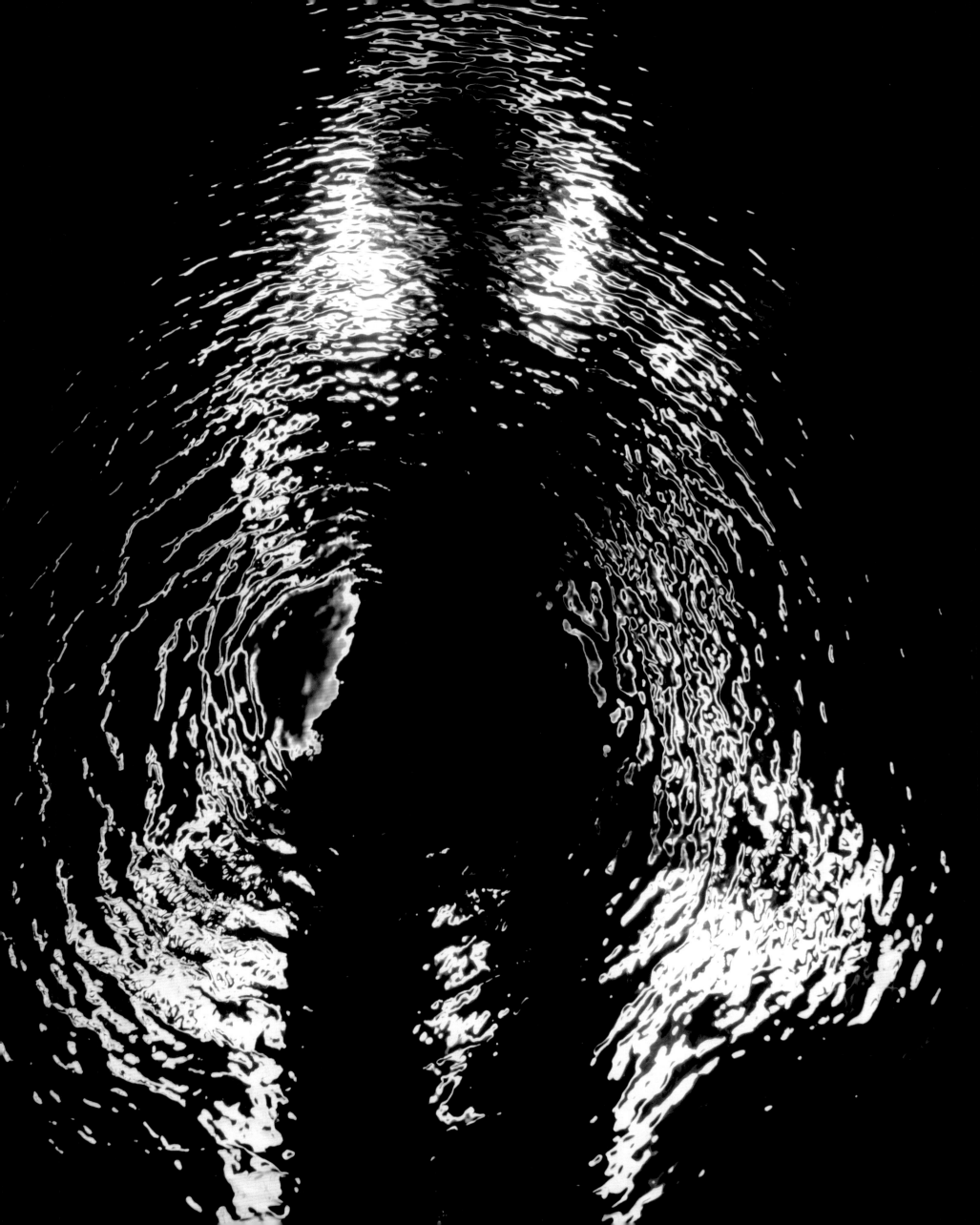

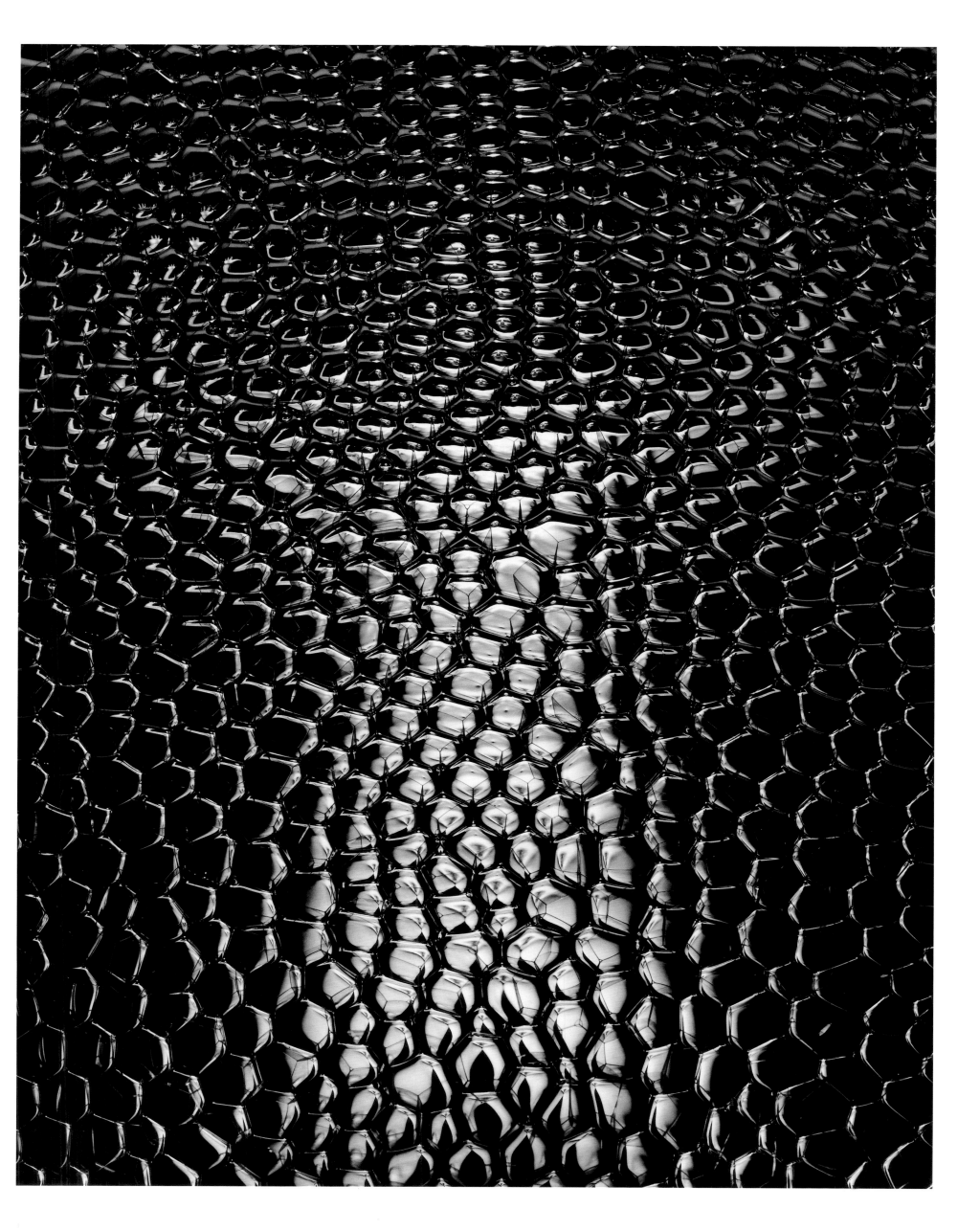

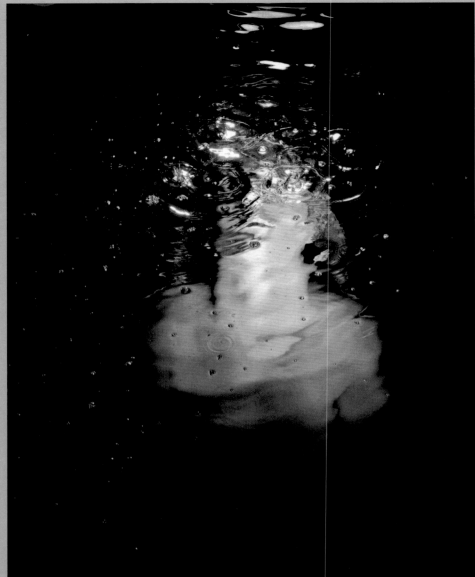

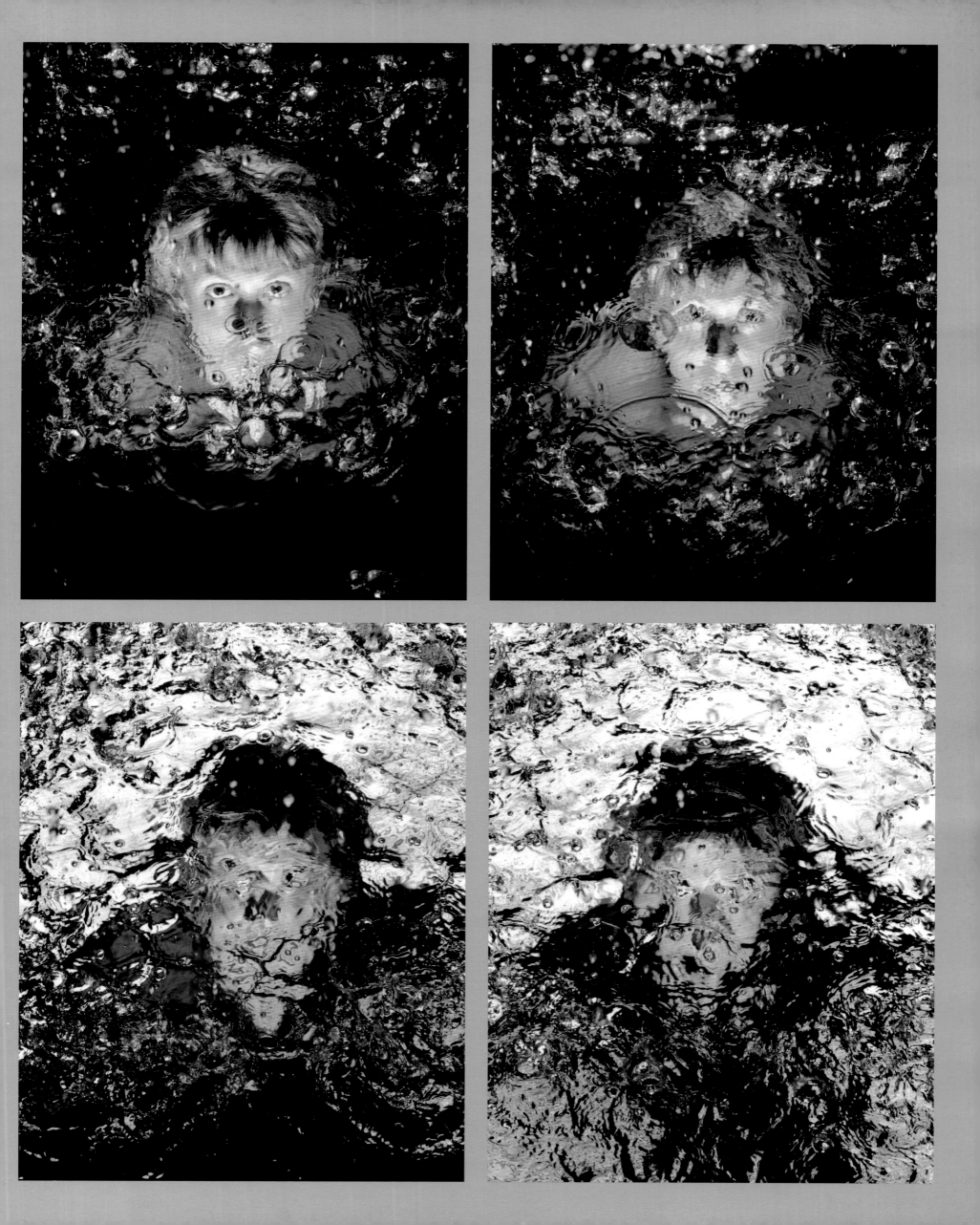

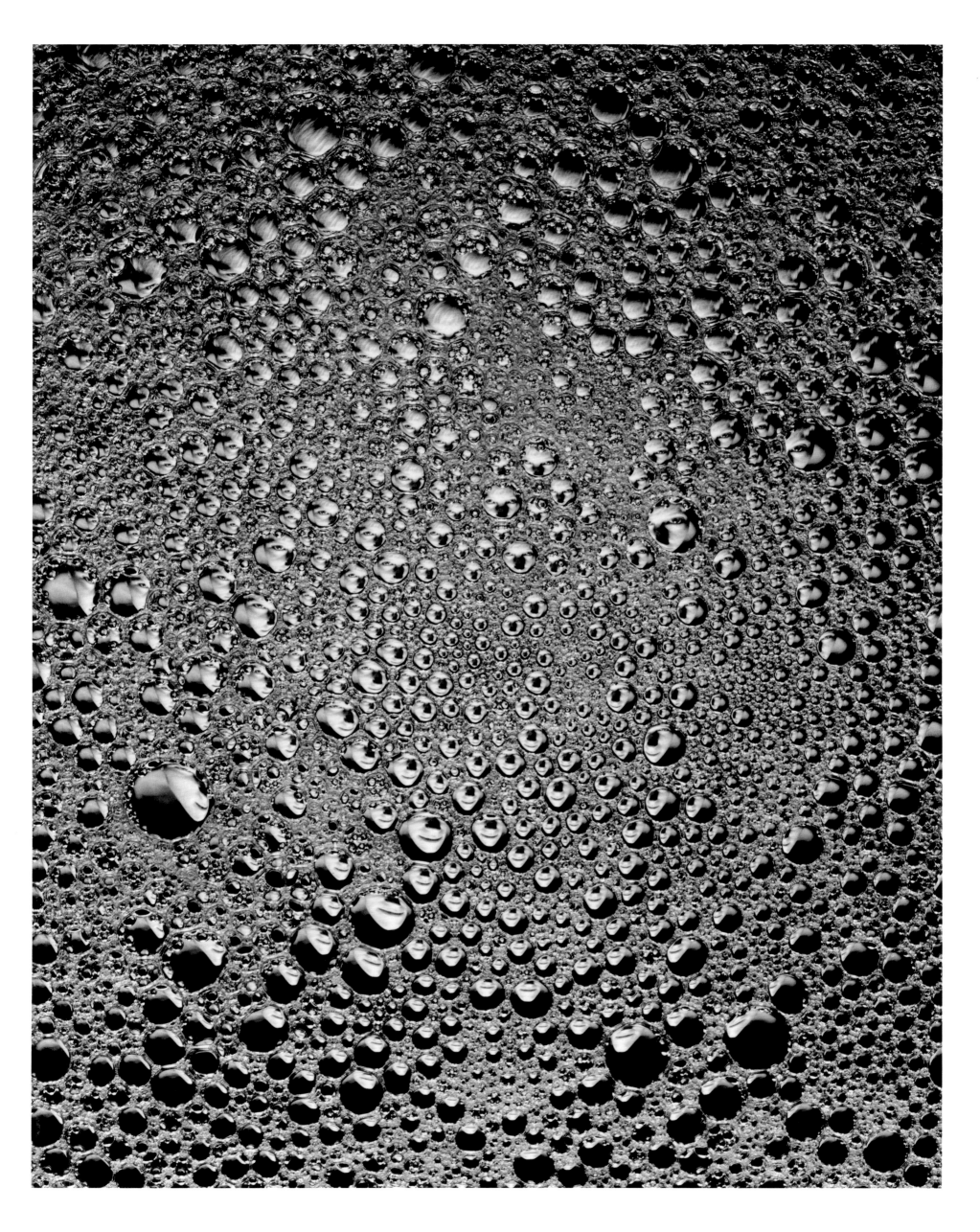

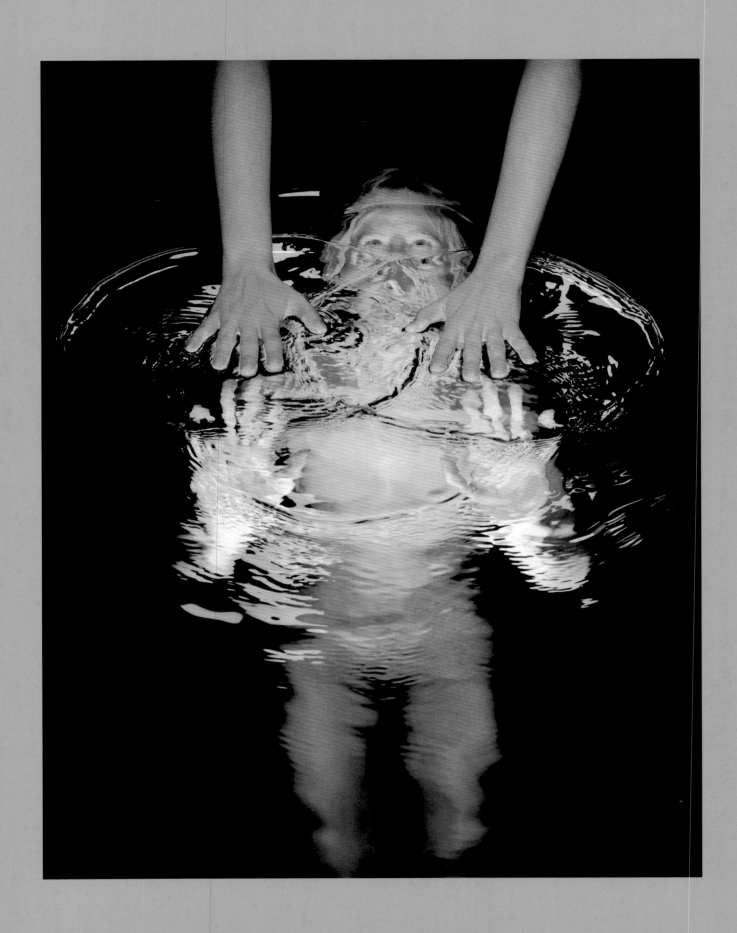

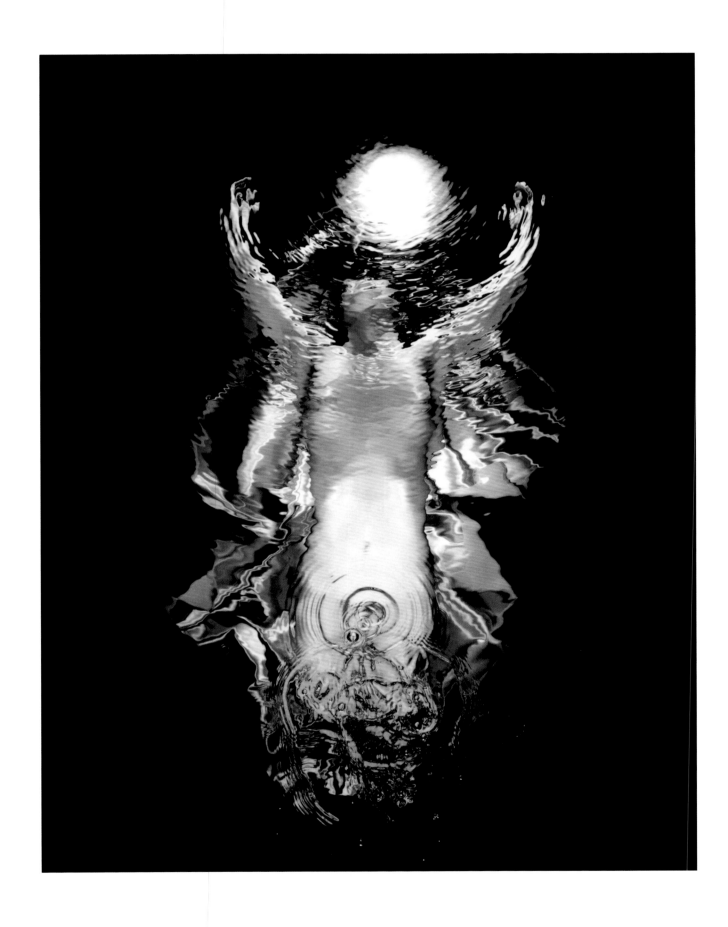

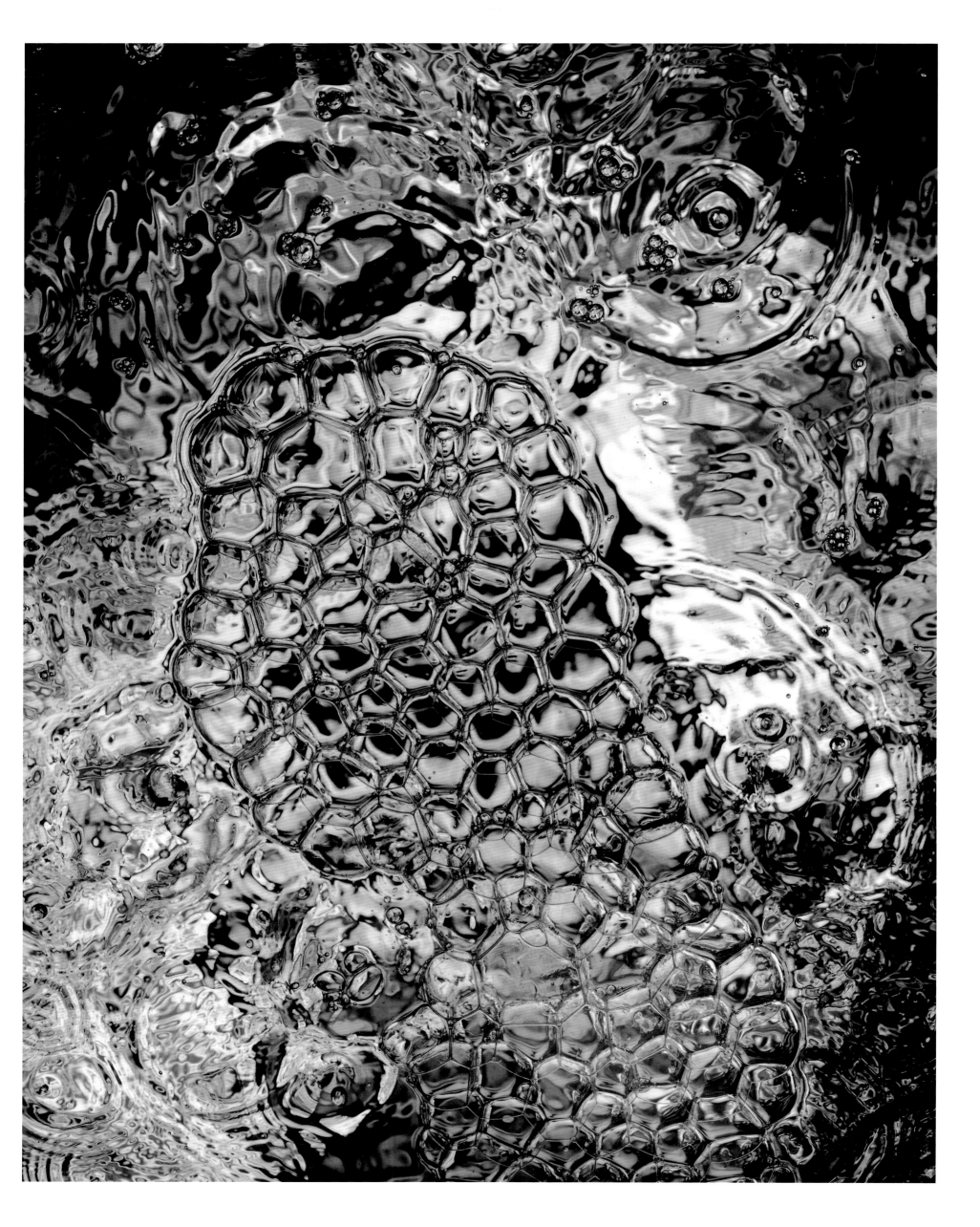

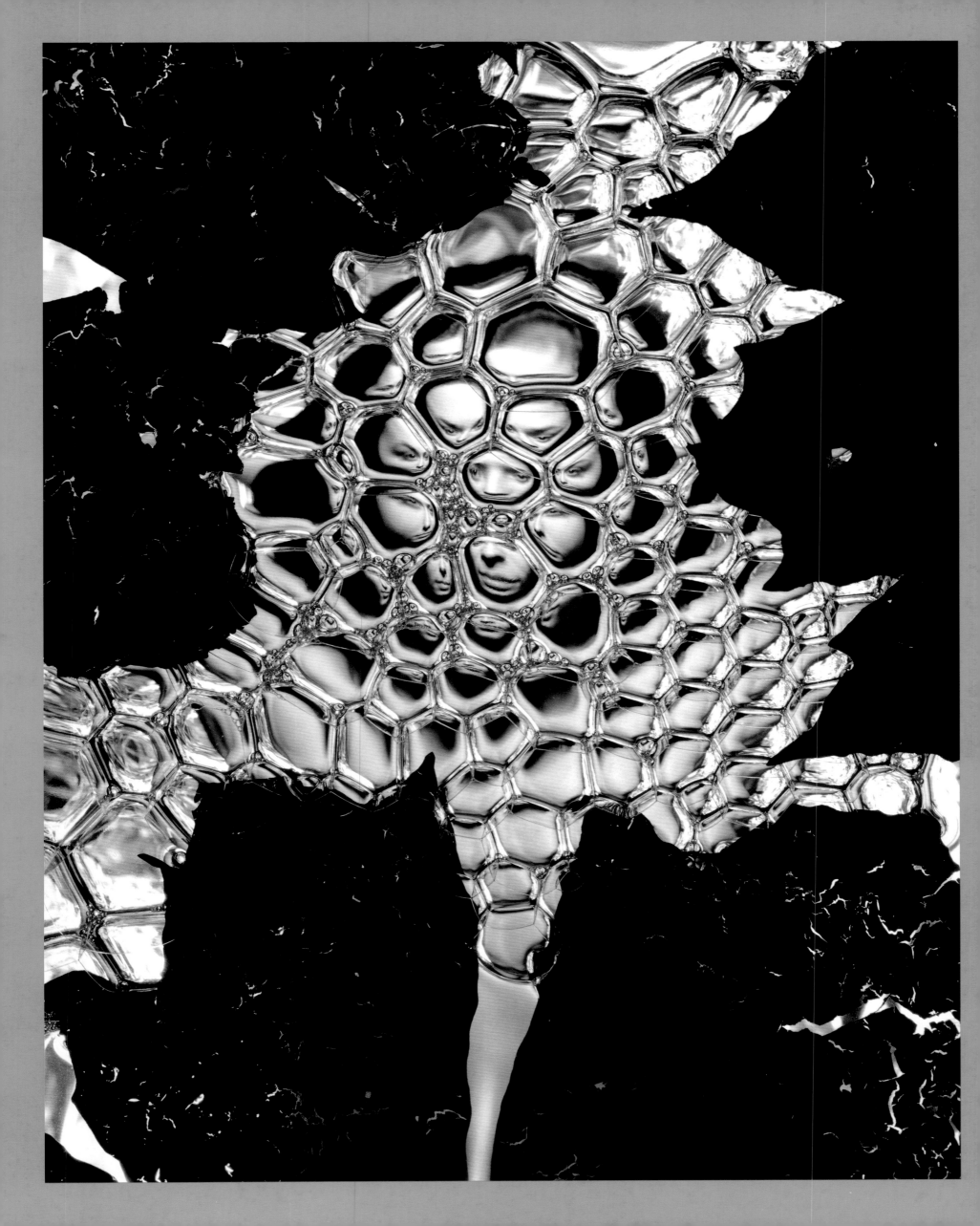

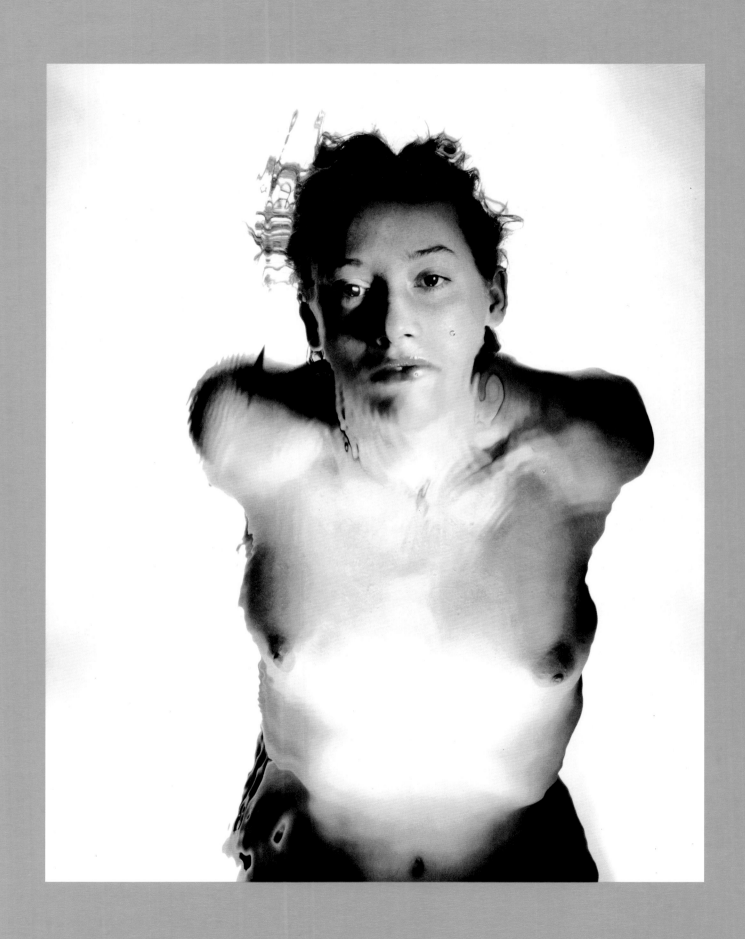

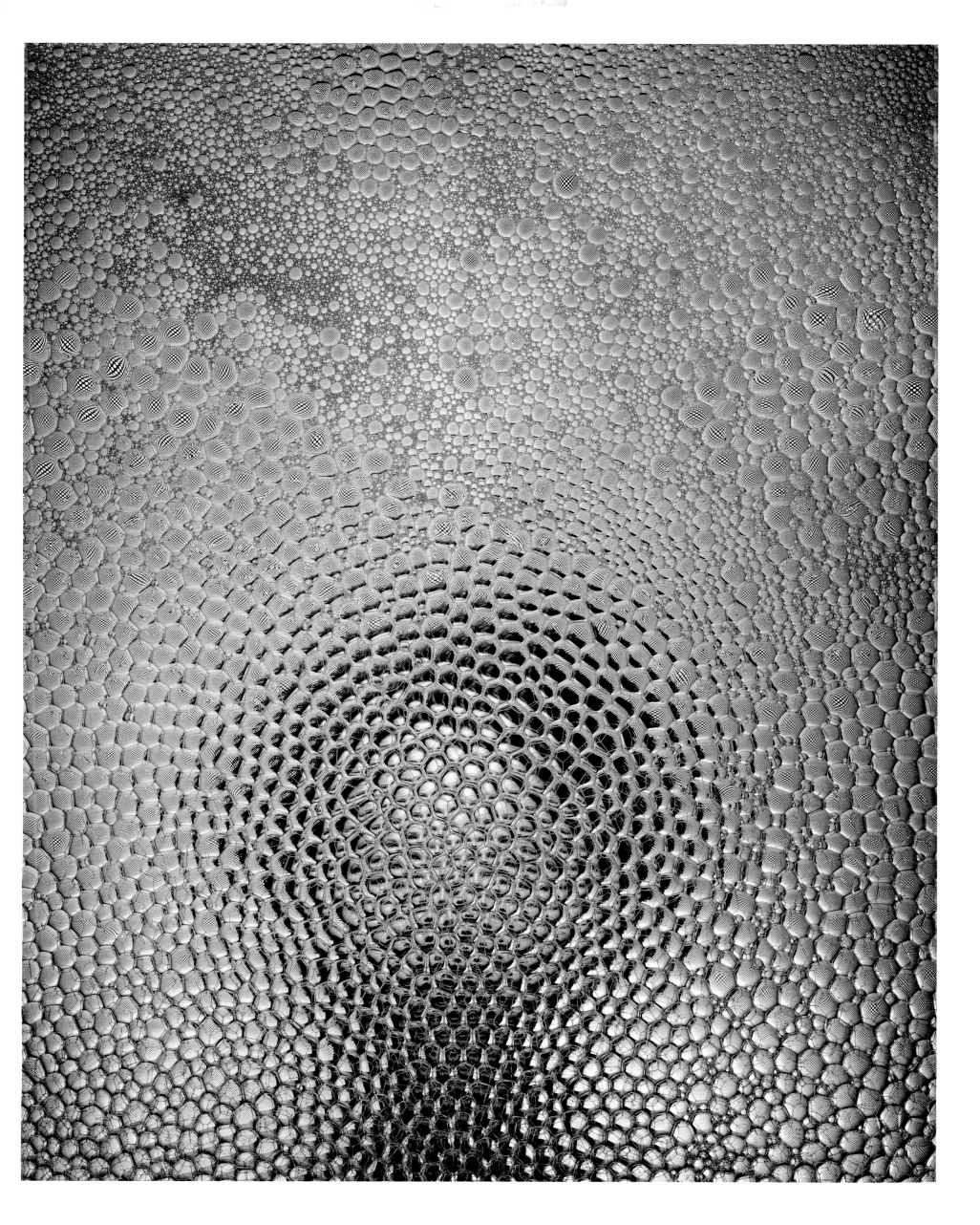

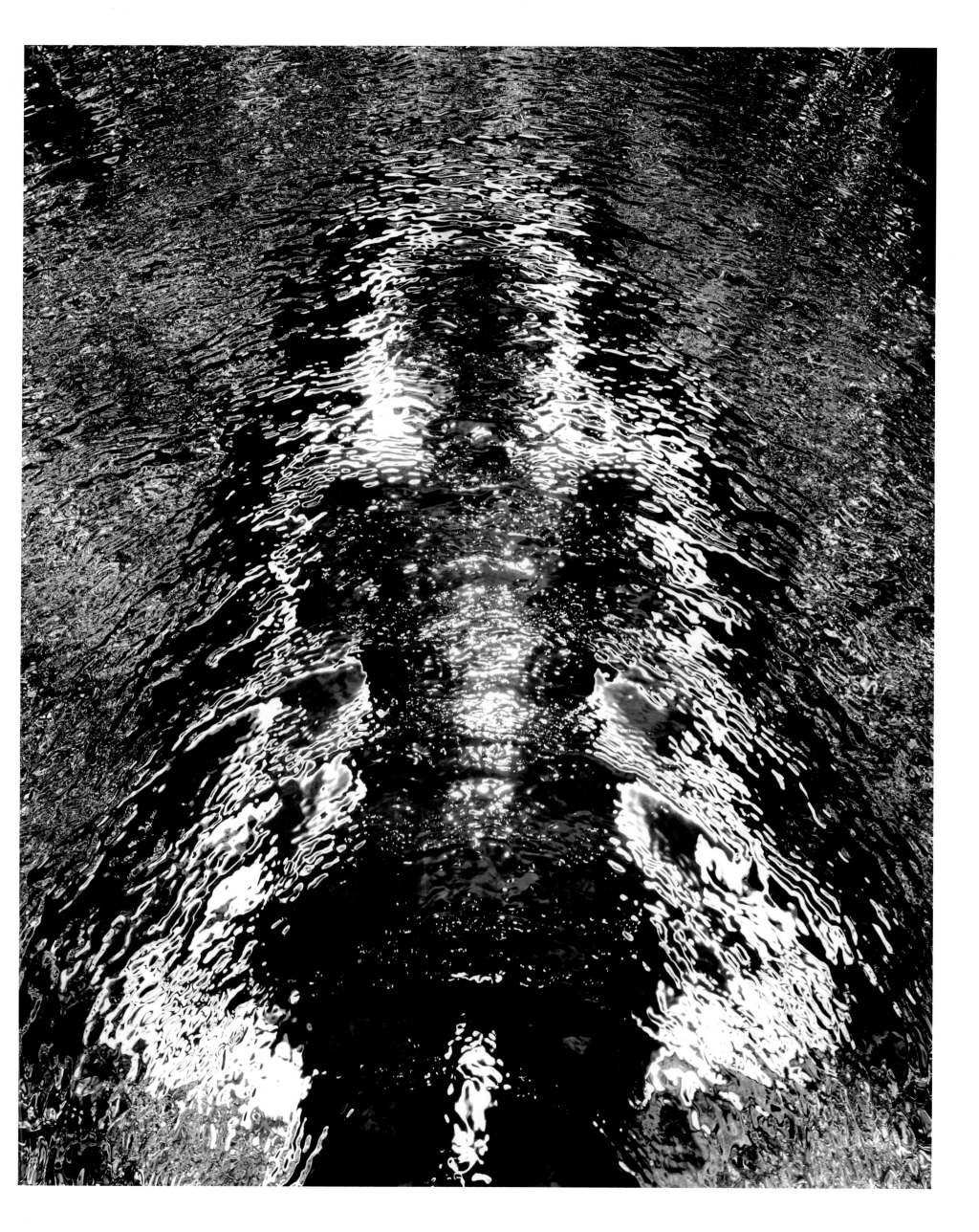

EVOLUTION

WS-00 1993

The photograph that started it all. As I make pictures, I try to keep an open mind and let my work have a voice in its own progression. Looking at—and listening to—this image after it was done, I thought, "What if these objects, suspended in air above the figure, actually were floating in water?"

WS-01 1993 ❋ Page 15

My first attempt to create a natural-looking body of water in the studio. Having thought about the visual characteristics of water in nature, I provided a reflection of sky and leaves, some wind, and a little splash. I was pleased with the result, but saw it only as an experiment. I was not planning to pursue this idea or expand it into a large series.

WS-02 1995 ❋ Page 75

Sometime later, I tried again, emphasizing the hands of the model. In this, and the next two (WS-03 and 04), a representation of an idealized Nature was still my intention. I added foliage to provide a referent to a natural environment.

WS-03 1995 ❋ Page 51

WS-04 1995 ❋ Page 19

Viewed chronologically, the *Water Series* has progressed as an exploration of one idea followed by another in a linear way, interspersed with occasional revisitations of earlier themes. The pictures I'm working on at the time always serve as breeding grounds for further experiments.

WS-05 1995 ❋ Page 34

Utilizing the same set and model as WS-04, here I reversed the tonality of the figure and the background. This reversal is something I continue to do throughout the course of the series.

WS-06 1995 ❋ Page 129

In this picture, one of the more elaborate—or determined—attempts to create the illusion of a natural setting, I started to work with the idea of the figure interacting with the surface of the water. I had begun to realize that the surface—and the worlds above and below it—was a fascinating arena to explore, full of energy, symbolism, and tension.

WS-07 1995 ❋ Page 17

A variation of WS-06, employing the same set but with a different arrangement of key elements. I work very experimentally, empirically perhaps. I don't always have a complete preconception, and am often surprised by the journey the picture leads me on. I usually photograph the same model in the same set over a number of days; what emerges sometimes astonishes me.

 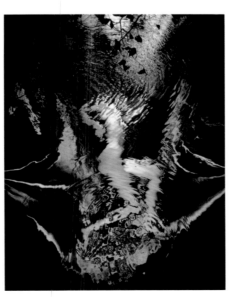  

WS-08 1995 ❋ Page 22

This picture was exhibited at the Albright-Knox Art Gallery in 1997, which set off a chain of events precipitated by its use in a brochure. That led to a show at the Benton Museum of Art in Connecticut, which led to an exhibition at the Fay Gold Gallery in Atlanta, which in turn led to Emanuel Volakis' gallery in Yountville, California, where a subsequent show led to the publication of this book.

WS-09 1995 ❋ Page 20

Also exhibited at the Albright-Knox in 1997. Before that exhibition, the prints I had made were 11 × 14 inches. The curator encouraged me to make bigger prints (16 × 20 inches), and, when I enlarged this one, little figures refracted in some bubbles in the lower part of the image became visible. I found this very intriguing and resolved to explore that phenomenon later in greater depth.

WS-10 1995 ❋ Page 25

With WS-09 through 12, I began working with a broader, deeper pool, which allowed for different kinds of illusion. The camera is farther away and sees a broader range; the figure is smaller, surrounded by more water; and their relative proportions carry a different aesthetic than in previous works.

WS-11 1995 ❋ Page 32

WS-12 1995 ✦ PAGE 106

Like WS-11, a larger set and deeper water.

WS-13 1995 ✦ PAGE 16

In another experiment, here I wanted to see what might happen if there were two figures interacting from both sides of the water.

WS-14 1996

The first of several pictures that depart from the attempt to mimic Nature and begin to isolate attention on the face. I also began exploring the visual effects and potentials of the optics of water, particularly water in motion.

WS-14B 1996 ✦ PAGE 114

WS-15 1996 ✦ PAGE 4

Another picture that isolates the face under the water. This was my first deliberate attempt to bring bubbles into an image, an idea that had come from their serendipitous introduction in WS-09. Working on this picture I got a first inkling of how difficult their manufacture was going to be, and that some significant engineering would be required.

WS-16 1997 ✦ PAGE 134

There is something both mystical and mythical about the symmetry of the human form, a notion I explored in WS-17 and 18 as well.

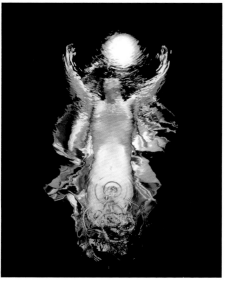

WS-17 1997 ✦ PAGE 92

I often don't know where a picture is going to lead when I start out with only a nascent idea or rough sketch. It takes over; it has a life of its own and sometimes tells me where to go next. My works are not really manifestations of the revelations of poetic musings, rather a series of visual what-ifs.

WS-18 1998 ✦ PAGE 23

Throughout the *Water Series*, the focus of the camera almost never leaves the surface of the water. Here, an inquisitive gaze is wrapped in watery folds.

WS-19 1998 ✦ PAGE 68

The first attempt at a large amount of turbulence and lensing bubbles, which interact with the body below. As a consequence, the image becomes more abstract; the figure, like a constellation.

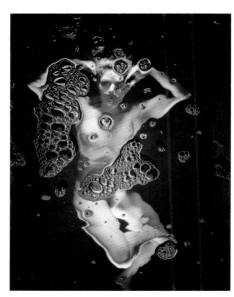

WS-20 1998 ✦ PAGE 60

A group of pictures (with WS-21 through 24) that explores the figure interacting optically with groups of bubbles. Bubbles have a physics all their own, with visual lensing manifestations far beyond the expectable.

WS-21 1998 ✦ PAGE 105

WS-22 1998 ✦ PAGE 45

Along with WS-23 and 24, these pictures show a multiplicity of images in which groups of lensing bubbles cross the surface of the water above the face. They were a result of many hours of experimenting with—and mining the possibilities of—the optical properties of various surfactants. One first notices the calligraphy of the figure, then the cluster of bubbles repeating the face.

WS-23 1998 ☼ Page 95

WS-24 1998 ☼ Page 94

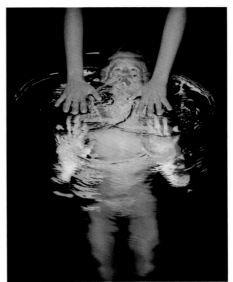

WS-25 #2 1999 ☼ Page 84

Another attempt at combining two figures interacting at the surface of the water, a revisiting of an idea first explored in WS-13. The surface represents a manifold, a layer of illumination separating the physical and the spiritual. Here are resolutely physical limbs in the air and a mysterious, otherworldly figure underneath.

WS-25 #4 1999 ☼ Page 85

WS-26 1999 ☼ Page 111

Combining some ideas from recent predecessors, this picture works with turbulence, bubbles, and human symmetry to project power and strength.

WS-27 1999 ☼ Page 149

The first picture in which I began to test waveforms and how they interact and interfere with each other.

WS-28 1999 ☼ Page 56

WS-29 1999 ☼ Page 61

WS-29 through 33 make a group that combines (and changes) the ideas manifested in the immediately preceding pictures. I reversed the tonality of the figure and background from black to white (as in WS-21 through 24), and substituted waveforms for bubbles.

WS-30 1999 ☼ Page 54

WS-31 1999 ☼ Page 86

Here and in WS-33, I was surprised to see how reversing the tonality from earlier studies (WS-20 and 24) made the figure appear to be made of some sort of metallic liquid; the water itself seems invisible.

WS-32 1999 ☼ Page 39

Another idea: a strong directional blast of air.

WS-33 1999 ☼ Page 87

WS-34 1999 ☀ PAGE 46

For the first time in the *Water Series*, the camera, from below, looks up through the water into the air. I return to using elements such as trees and foliage to imply a setting in Nature.

WS-35 1999 ☀ PAGE 47

The model creates waves in the water.

WS-37 1999 ☀ PAGE 122

WS-38 1999 ☀ PAGE 123

An enigmatic figure at water's edge.

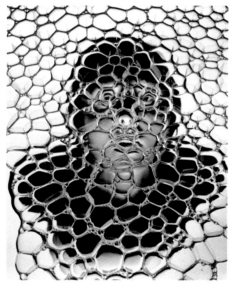

WS-39 1999 ☀ PAGE 43

After much experimentation, I discovered a way to manufacture a uniform sheet of bubbles. It took several days to make the apparatus work. Here the camera looks down through lensing bubbles to a mysteriously deconstructed face.

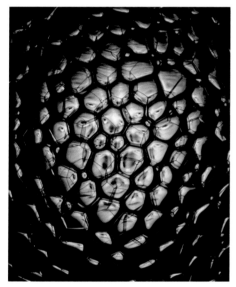

WS-40 1999 ☀ PAGE 7

Reverse the tonality of the face and background and make a sheet of larger bubbles: the image is even more abstracted. Here, as in WS-39, the discrete and amazing structure of the bubbles is made visible. I soon realized that to be able to see the increasingly fine detail, my prints would have to be larger still. I began making them 20 × 24 inches.

WS-41 1999 ☀ PAGE 71

Another, larger field of bubbles with the figure seen almost in entirety. Every single bubble contains an image of the complete figure, each from a slightly different angle. From a distance, a barely discernable figure; a little nearer, an abstract pattern; closer still, a myriad of figures.

WS-42 1999 ☀ PAGE 108

Back to turbulence in the water and a dynamic representation of the figure seen from below. Working with water in the studio can be very demanding, and I sometimes take a break from one sort of picture to work on a very different idea; this one is reminiscent of the images in WS-29 through 33, save that the camera is now back below the surface.

WS-43 1999 ☀ PAGE 69

A complete figure is seen through a manifold of lensing bubbles.

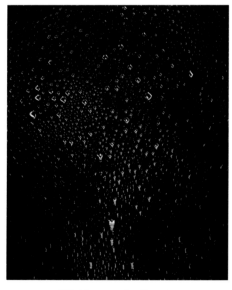

WS-44 1999 ☀ PAGE 49

Rather than a field or sheet of uniform bubbles, this surface (and those of WS-44 #2 and #3) employs tiny, random bubble lenses to reproduce the figure from literally thousands of viewpoints. Astronomical in perspective, it is the "telescopic" equivalent of the WS-41 "microscopic" view. (This was the era of the first Hubble Deep Field photograph, so I called this, naturally, the Bubble Deep Field.)

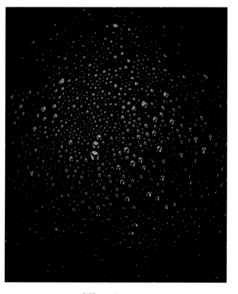

WS-44#2 1999

WS-44#3 1999 ☀ PAGE 103

WS-44A 1999

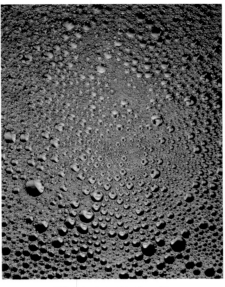

WS-45 1999 ☼ PAGE 83

This is somewhat similar to WS-44 in the way it was made, only with some of the light illuminating the bubbles themselves, rendering them shadowed, dimensional, and filled with faces. Since the first time I laid eyes on it, this image always hypnotizes me.

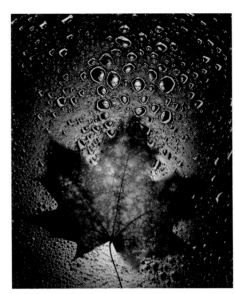

WS-46 1999 ☼ PAGE 59

Before the *Water Series* began, I had been making photographic "portraits" of leaves. I continue to use them in my work; here, a maple leaf, surrounded by small bubble-lens images of a face.

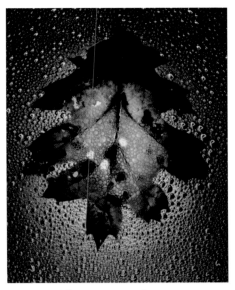

WS-47 1999 ☼ PAGE 113

An oak leaf floating in an atmosphere of tiny figures.

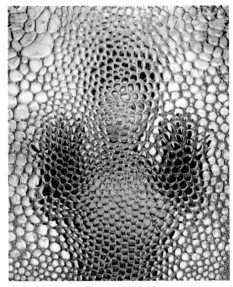

WS-48 1999 ☼ PAGE 38

Somewhat similar to WS-41, but with a white background. Another reversal of figure/ground tonality.

WS-49 1999 ☼ PAGE 101

A unique image in the series: a clinging cluster of bubbles creates a peninsula of distorted faces tossing on roiling water.

WS-50 1999 ☼ PAGE 44

WS-51 1999 ☼ PAGE 104

A field of bubbles showing multiple views of a face surrounded by enormous leaves in silhouette, creating a palette of negative space.

WS-54 1999 ☼ PAGE 63

As with so many *Water Series* photographs, effects I hadn't imagined emerge. The figure in this picture makes me think of classical Roman statuary.

WS-56 2000 ☼ PAGE 55

Seen from below, an energized figure swirls her long hair in the water.

WS-56 #9 2000 ☼ PAGE 97

WS-57 2000 ☼ PAGE 30

With the camera below the surface, the figure moves the water from a mysterious dark.

WS-58 2000 ✸ PAGE 27

In a natural environment seen in a supernatural way, a face floats in the reflected sky, a splashing leaf in the foreground.

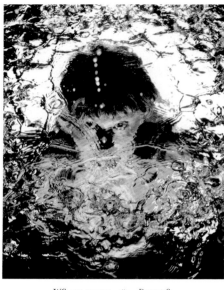

WS-59 2000 ✸ PAGE 78

One of a group of photographs showing a face through "rain" on water, a theme I keep returning to (WS-59 through 61).

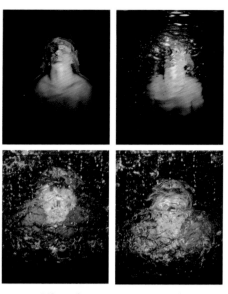

WS-59-61#1 2000 ✸ PAGE 76

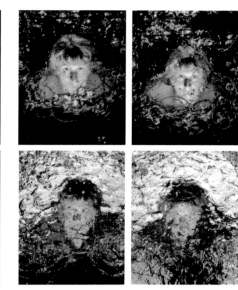

WS-59-61#2 2000 ✸ PAGE 77

WS-61 2000 ✸ PAGE 79

WS-62#6 2000 ✸ PAGE 72

This picture evokes in me a feeling I sometimes get from certain images from the Italian Renaissance.

WS-65#7 2001 ✸ PAGE 36

The first family of pictures (WS-66 and 67) in which I used a patterned background behind the figure. A strong blast of air moves the water, then leaves a calm spot where, perhaps, an eye shows through.

WS-66#3 2001

WS-67#2 2001 ✸ PAGE 52

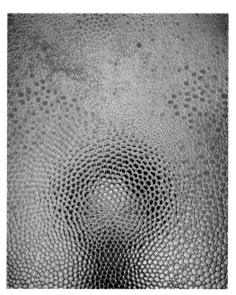

WS-69#6 2001 ✸ PAGE 91

This picture (as in WS-69 and 70) uses bubbles over a pattern of dots, making for an amazing Op-Art explosion.

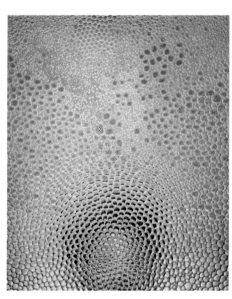

WS-69#7 2001 ✸ PAGE 133

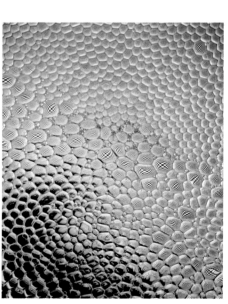

WS-70#2 2001 ✸ PAGE 29

WS-71 #10 2001 ☼ PAGE 127

WS-71 through 73 employ a layer of stripes interacting with
the water to create strong moire patterns in the background,
complementing the powerfully mysterious spirits implied
by the figures.

WS-72 #3 2001 ☼ PAGE 126

WS-72 #4 2001 ☼ PAGE 37

WS-72 #7 2001 ☼ PAGE 89

WS-72 #16 2001 ☼ PAGE 24

WS-73 #5 2001 ☼ PAGE 117

WS-74 #4 2001 ☼ PAGE 65

Combining a patterned background, leaves, and blasts of air
to sculpt the surface of the water, this image, with its half-
moon face, was chosen as the cover of this book.

WS-75 #5 2001 ☼ PAGE 35

The first work to employ an engine designed to "shake"
the water, thereby making a regular pattern on its surface.
A rheostat adjusts the degree of vibration the device will
impart to the tank. I used this technique also in
WS-77, 85, and 109.

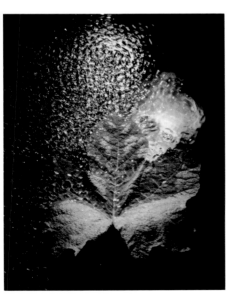

WS-77 #5 2001 ☼ PAGE 31

An arrangement of shaking water, a beautiful leaf,
and a face.

WS-78 #13 2001 ☼ PAGE 109

Competing wave fronts, a strong figure,
and crocheted lace in the background.

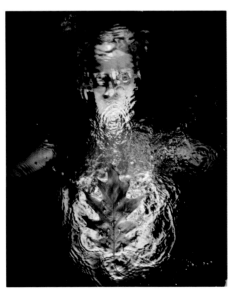

WS-82 #1 2002 ☼ PAGE 123

Back to the purity of nature, sort of. A figure with a leaf that
had just been dropped in the water. Though practiced at
controlling the dynamics of a picture, I am often
(and happily) surprised by the results.
Here the leaf became a rib cage.

WS-83 #4 2002 ☼ PAGE 124

A reversal of the tonality of the figure and
background in WS-82 #1.

WS-83#6 2002 ☀ PAGE 98

A leaf, a figure, and a serendipitous pattern of drops that
had not yet hit the surface when they were captured on film.
I felt as soon as I saw it that I would never again capture
a moment like that. So far, I've been right.

WS-84#2 2002 ☀ PAGE 115

So much of my work at this time involved trying to create
dramatic effects in the water's surface—a result of precise
timing, a choreography among the model, the water, the
equipment, the camera, and myself—that a photograph such
as this one, with its ethereal subtleties, went unnoticed and
unappreciated until I was re-examining my work for this
book. I now find this image, similar to WS-14B, of my best.

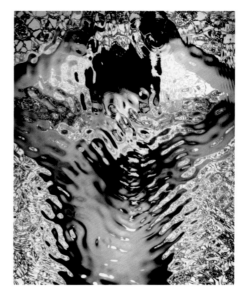

WS-85 2002 ☀ PAGE 116

Shake the water just right and you get twelve eyes.

WS-86#16 2000 ☀ PAGE 96

Striped background and concentric ringed waves produce,
again, a moire Op-Art pattern. With the same set and model
as WS-85, a different shape to the surface of the water and
a different background produce strikingly
dissimilar results.

WS-88#11 2002 ☀ PAGE 73

The simple elements of this image reveal themselves to be
complex and dense.

WS-89#9 2002 ☀ PAGE 131

In this picture, Queen Anne's lace floats over
a figure in the water.

WS-90#13 2003 ☀ PAGE 66

Though some see intimations of characters from classic
myths and stories, my figures are spirits, and the water represents an ethereal, not literally aquatic, realm.
The work is meant to be celebratory.

WS-92 2003 ☀ PAGE 135

WS-94#10 2004 ☀ PAGE 80

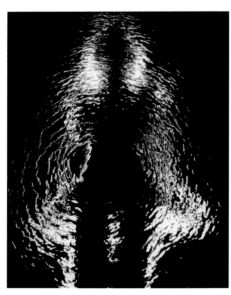

WS-95#7 2004 ☀ PAGE 57

A background baffle is lit from below, producing what
seems an electric "aura."

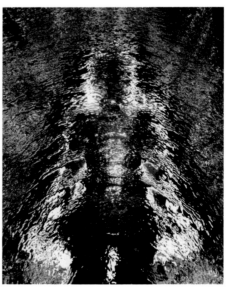

WS-96#14 2004 ☀ PAGE 137

WS-97#9 2004 ☀ PAGE 33

Complicated patterns swirl around a Pharaonic figure.

WS-98 2005 ✷ PAGE 67

A classic pose in an atmospheric pool.

WS-99.3#10 2005 ✷ PAGE 119

While working on this picture I found I couldn't escape a serendipitous but strong evocation of medieval religious imagery.

WS-100.3#17 2005 ✷ PAGE 40

A figure conjuring magic in a smoke-like water.

WS-101.2 2005 ✷ PAGE 93

WS-104 2006 ✷ PAGE 121

A unique photograph in the *Water Series*—the only picture to date with the figure and the camera on the same side of the water — and the only one which consciously references a classical theme. Its imagery is based on classical works showing water as the source and fount of life.

WS-107 2006 ✷ PAGE 81

The interplay of light, shadow, and pose make this seem almost a portrait.

WS-108 2006 ✷ PAGE 50

Bright beams radiate from a dynamic, expressive figure.

WS-109.4#6 2006 ✷ PAGE 41

Light glows below silhouetted hands in an environment of watery patterns. The tank is being shaken to create a surprisingly energetic field around the figure.

WS-110.2#14 2006 ✷ PAGE 21

In this picture and the one that follows, the figure seems to be in and on the water at the same time.

WS-111#6 2006 ✷ PAGE 107

"When people ask how I make my photographs I say, "think layers." I work to make my pictures reveal themselves slowly, as they possess different levels. Light, pattern, figure, water, light, camera, viewer. Some layers reveal themselves only upon re-viewing or when studying larger prints. Some layers become apparent only after time has passed. Convinced that photography's power comes from its unparalleled ability to describe what's visible in front of the camera, I try to provide subjects, or combinations of light and substance, to test that power. Pictures in the *Water Series* proclaim: there it is, but it can't be, but there it is; an energized, subconscious dialogue between picture and viewer. You may be looking up when you think you're looking down. Even though these images are unmanipulated photographs, they can have great mystery about what they are. The studio is my laboratory, where I work to present subtle evidence that something is impossible; and yet there it, unquestionably, is."

BIOGRAPHY

Brian Oglesbee was born in Chicago in 1951, and first became interested in photography in the sixth grade when he and his father built a pinhole camera together for a science project. He attended J. Sterling Morton East High School in Cicero, Illinois, which had an incomparable four-year photography program led by Edward Sturr, a graduate of the legendary Institute of Design program at the Illinois Institute of Technology. While still in high school he began working in commercial studios in Chicago. Oglesbee then attended the Art Institute of Chicago, where he studied etching and photoengraving with Vera Berdich and photomechanical printmaking with Sonia Sheridan, and collaborated on artist's books with Keith Smith.

After a career as a commercial photographer for the Vogue-Wright Studios in Chicago, at that time the country's largest commercial photography studio, he moved to upstate New York, where he taught photography and printmaking at Alfred University. During the 1980s he became known for a series of large-format photographs of room scenes and still lifes, and began to develop techniques and equipment to fulfill his personal vision of what photography could be.

In 1993, Oglesbee was granted a U.S. patent for the invention of his Photographic Studio System, an array of modular components for set-building, camera support, and lighting control.

Oglesbee has been widely exhibited in one-person and group shows throughout the United States, Europe, and Japan, and is represented in collections in such institutions as the George Eastman House (Rochester, NY), the International Center of Photography (New York, NY), the Museum of Fine Arts (St. Petersburg, FL), the Musee de l'Elysee (Lausanne, Switzerland), the Museum of Fine Arts (Houston, TX), the Brooklyn Museum (Brooklyn, NY), and many private collections, including the Sir Elton John Collection (Atlanta, GA). He has given presentations of his work throughout the United States, and has twice been granted fellowships by the New York Foundation for the Arts.

His work has been included in *Face: The New Photographic Portrait*, *Flora Photographica: Masterpieces of Flower Photography*, and *The Joy of Digital Photography*. Portfolios of his work have appeared in *View Camera*, *American Photo*, *Photo/Design*, and *Metropolitan Home*, among other magazines.

From 1986 to the present, Oglesbee has maintained a studio in Wellsville, New York, where he lives with his wife, Mandy. For the past eleven years, Oglesbee has worked almost exclusively on the *Water Series (Aquatique)*.

ACKNOWLEDGMENTS

First and foremost, I must pay homage to all those who have so graciously facilitated this work by modeling for me. For your hours spent in a world of too hot lights, too wet water, and too cold air—in sometimes precarious positions—and being asked to endure too many repetitions as we worked out the choreography of pose and light with the movement of the water, I am deeply grateful. It would not have been possible without you.

Having hardly ever let an opportunity pass without encouraging me to pursue the creation of a book of these images, William Edwards deserves special thanks for his years of support, help, and advice. Photographer and writer Jeff Wignall is another longtime supporter and encourager who has enthusiastically endured hours of conversation in regards to the *Water Series* and this project, and who has patiently doled out good advice and help. Similarly, I have to thank Megan and Les Brill for their many years of support, friendship, and enlightened criticism.

This book would not have been possible without Emanuel Dimitri Volakis. I thank him for his persistence in convincing me to become a part of Volakis Gallery, and his willingness to risk flying such a skeptic out to California to print very large silver prints in his amazing darkroom, because he knew this work had to be big. Without his premonition, appreciation, stewardship, and support the publishers would not have had occasion to meet my work.

I feel I owe a debt of gratitude to my most important teachers as well. First among them would be my father, John W. Oglesbee, whose lifelong interest in photography is surely what got me started. In high school I had the good fortune to have met a brilliant teacher, Edward Sturr, who set the bar high and provided the perfect example of a serious artist and photographer. He continues to be a strong influence on me and my work. In art school I had another teacher, Keith Smith, who continues to be a source of inspiration. As he has been the creator of over 250 artist books, I hope he can find some small thing to appreciate in this one.

Special thanks to Lesley Brill, for his insightful thoughts and thoughtful insights.

Among the people I should also like to thank for their longtime support, help, and understanding are Pete Lekousis and Geophrey Wilber in Chicago, William Underhill in Wellsville, Amy Miller in Atlanta, Ed Rose in Boston, Max Oglesbee in New York, and Phoebe Oglesbee in Wellsville.

How fortunate I am to have had the opportunity to collaborate with the wonderful people at Insight Editions. Thank you, Michael Madden, Robbie Schmidt, and Raoul Goff, for your inspiration, patience and "Insight." Thank you, Mark Burstein, for your careful editing and help in polishing words; Iain Morris for your brilliant design; and Mikayla Butchart for all your help.

Lastly, my most important advisor, trusted critic, and sounding board in this work has been the artist and painter Amanda Parry Oglesbee, my wife, to whom this book is dedicated with gratitude, admiration, and love.

COLOPHON

Publisher & Creative Director: *Raoul Goff*
Executive Directors: *Michael Madden & Peter Beren*
Art Director & Designer: *Iain R. Morris*
Acquiring Editor: *Mikayla Butchart*
Production Director: *Susan Ristow*
Production Manager: *Lina Palma*
Studio Production Manager & Press Supervisor: *Noah Potkin*
Project Editor: *Mark Burstein*
Managing Editors: *Emanuel Volakis & Jennifer Gennari*

The display type in *Aquatique* uses Trade Gothic, a classic, modulated sans-serif font.
The first cuts of Trade Gothic were designed by Jackson Burke in 1948.

The body of the book is set in Mrs. Eaves, a digital font designed by Zuzana Licko in 1996 as an historical revival based Baskerville. This typeface, a modern serif that retains an air of antiquated dignity, is named after Sarah Eaves, the woman who became John Baskerville's wife and a printer in her own right.

The book was printed using a quadtone process employing four layers of ink: two blacks, a special warm gray, and a metallic. A dry-tapped spot gloss varnish was used to preserve the density of the original prints. Color separations and printing were carried out by using 250 line screen.

INSIGHT EDITIONS

Insight Editions
17 Paul Drive
San Rafael, CA, 94903
415.526.1370

www.insighteditions.com

Library of Congress Cataloging-in-Publication Data available

ISBN-13: 978-1-933784-15-5
Limited Edition ISBN-13: 978-1-933784-43-4

Palace Press International, in association with Global ReLeaf, will plant two trees for each tree used in the manufacturing of this book. Global ReLeaf is an international campaign by American Forests, the nation's oldest nonprofit conservation organization and a world leader in planting trees for environmental restoration.

Brian Oglesbee's photographs are represented by
Volakis Gallery
6730 Washington Street
Yountville, CA 94599
www.volakisgallery.com

10 9 8 7 6 5 4 3 2 1

Printed in China by Palace Press International

www.palacepress.com